Original title:
Laughs in the Latticework

Copyright © 2025 Creative Arts Management OÜ
All rights reserved.

Author: Liam Sterling
ISBN HARDBACK: 978-1-80567-424-5
ISBN PAPERBACK: 978-1-80567-723-9

Twirls of Humor in Every Fiber

In the garden of jesters, we twirl and spin,
With giggles and chuckles, we wear our grin.
A tickle of mirth in the morning light,
As shadows of laughter dance through the night.

Each fabric of fun seams joy into lace,
We skip over puddles, our worries erase.
With every small stumble, we burst into cheer,
The world is a canvas, let laughter be near.

Reflections of Joyful Moments

Mirrors of laughter reflect in our eyes,
With each little joke, a balloon in the skies.
We gather our smiles, like petals in spring,
Twirling and swirling - oh, joy that we bring!

In puddles of humor, we splash and we play,
The sun shines down brightly, come join in the fray.
With winks and a nudge, the world feels so bright,
Every tickle of joy is a spark of delight.

The Patchwork of Playfulness

With patches of colors, our laughter is sewn,
In the quilt of our memories, joy is well-known.
Threads of the playful weave stories so grand,
Together we journey, let's take a light stand.

In this fabric of glee, we find our own way,
With puns and clever jests, we brighten the day.
A hop and a skip bring us closer, so fun,
In the warmth of our laughter, we shine like the sun.

Entwined Tales of Happiness

In the fibers of tales where absurdity lurks,
We dance with our worries and twist them to quirks.
The rhythm of chuckles echoes and sways,
As we share silly stories that lighten our days.

Like vines that entwine in a joyful embrace,
We stumble, we fumble, but laughter finds place.
With a wink and a grin, let the nonsense unfold,
In this tapestry woven, pure joy to behold.

A Funny Stitch in Time

A needle winks, a fabric smiles,
Stitching tales through giggling miles.
Threads entwined in playful jest,
Every knot a clever quest.

Buttons dance with cheeky flair,
Tales of chaos fill the air.
Patchwork worlds where humor blooms,
Underneath the laughing looms.

Colorful Threads of Amusement

Bright colors spin and twirl around,
In this quilt where joy is found.
Hues of laughter, shades of cheer,
Woven tales for all to hear.

From silly patterns leap and dive,
In every stitch, the jokes arrive.
A tapestry of whimsy spun,
Knot by knot, we share the fun.

Sprightly Strands of Merriment

Twisted fibers, giddy and bright,
Chasing shadows, bouncing in light.
Threads that giggle as they play,
Merry mischief leads the way.

Dances of yarn in frolicsome glee,
Spinning tales both wild and free.
Every loop, a chuckle shared,
Crafting joy that's never bared.

Mirthful Notes in the Fabric

In woven lines, the laughter glows,
As every pattern freely flows.
A tapestry of funny dreams,
Where every stitch bursts at the seams.

Hilarious whispers in every fold,
Stories spun that never get old.
With every cut and every sew,
Joyful notes in the fabric flow.

Weaving Whispers of Mirth

In twinkling threads, the stories spin,
A tapestry where giggles begin,
Each knot a chuckle, each weave a grin,
Laughter echoes, inviting you in.

Beneath the beams, a dance of light,
Jest and jive in the soft twilight,
The spindle spins, joy taking flight,
In this realm, everything feels right.

Soft whispers weave through the open air,
Tickling senses with playful flair,
A tapestry rich with jokes to share,
Where mirth blooms free, beyond compare.

From frayed edges, the punchlines bloom,
Crafting bright tunes to dispel the gloom,
Each fiber a laugh, each turn a boom,
In this web of wit, we joyfully zoom.

Whispers Between the Threads

In a garden of giggles, secrets collide,
Woven stories where frolics hide.
Tickles of wind on a sunbeam's twist,
Frivolous dances in an air of mist.

Strings of laughter, cleverly spun,
Tangled up in playful fun.
Mirthful echoes in every seam,
We giggle beneath a daylight dream.

Twisted Shadows and Sunlit Grins

Shadows twist as sunlight spills,
Chasing silhouettes, the heart thrills.
Giant figures in a playful race,
With silly hats, we wear our grace.

Every chuckle spills like wine,
Refreshing sips with the sweetest brine.
Sunkissed joy in a fleeting glance,
Let's waltz again in this merry dance.

Echoes of Joy in Every Knothole

In the silence, a chuckle rings,
Spinning tales that laughter brings.
Hidden smiles in the wooden grain,
Whispers of fun may lighten pain.

Every knothole's a doorway wide,
To a world where the giggles abide.
Joy rides high on a playful breeze,
In the creaking wood, the heart finds ease.

Tangles of Humor and Heartstrings

Strings of fate are spun in jest,
Knotted laughter, the very best.
A ribbon of joy in a stormy sky,
Twists and turns as moments fly.

Pull on the threads, let the fun unfurl,
With every tug, see the humor swirl.
In the knots of life, we find our play,
As heartstrings dance, come what may.

The Raw Silk of Stories

In the corner, tales arise,
With wild dreams in playful guise.
Whispers twirl like threads in air,
Weaving smiles beyond compare.

A cat in socks, a dog in shoes,
Each tale a giggle, bright amuse.
They dance along the stroll of time,
In muted colors, yet they chime.

Grandpa's tales of sneaky pranks,
A mirror maze of giggly flanks.
The world unfolds in quirky schemes,
Where every laugh ignites our dreams.

A jacket worn on backward days,
A floppy hat that never sways.
These tales of old, like silken thread,
We stitch with joy, a laugh well-spread.

Vibrant Vines of Laughter

Bright vines twine in a sun-kissed glow,
Carrying giggles where breezes flow.
Tickling leaves whisper little plays,
In the garden where humor stays.

Chickens donning hats of style,
Pigs that pirouette with a smile.
Each creature sings a silly song,
Together, where we all belong.

Whimsical paths through green embrace,
Prancing squirrels in a funny race.
Nature's canvas, colors bright,
Brings forth laughter in pure delight.

Under the arch of joyful beams,
Life blossoms in ridiculous dreams.
With every twist and twisty turn,
We find the joy for which we yearn.

Carefree Patterns in the Loom

Patterns weave in colors bold,
Stories from the young and old.
Each thread a chuckle, spun with care,
Festive tales float in the air.

Clumsy dances, a shoe that slips,
Funny faces, comic quips.
Every stitch a tale retold,
In the fabric of fun we hold.

A sock bedecked in polka dots,
A teapot brewing teasing thoughts.
Such strings of joy that intertwine,
Creating chaos, simply divine.

Tangled yarns in a quirky mix,
Crafting stories with little tricks.
In our loom where laughter's play,
Spins a bright and happy day.

The Quilt of Quirkiness

Stitched together, patches bright,
Quirky moments shine with light.
A duck in boots, a frog in ties,
From every square, a big surprise.

Each snip and tuck a giggle blooms,
In cozy corners, joy resumes.
Layered laughter, warm and wide,
A treasure chest where quirks reside.

Polka dots on striped designs,
Whimsical shapes forming bright lines.
Together, they create a dance,
Inviting all to take a chance.

Tales unfold with every fold,
Old and new, the quilt grows bold.
In this patchwork of silly glee,
We find our joy in harmony.

Patterns of Light and Laughter

In the weave of day, a twist so bright,
A shadow leaps, brings sheer delight.
Every glimmer tells a tale,
Of mischief wrapped in a silver veil.

Giggles dance upon the breeze,
As sunlight plays among the trees.
A flicker here, a breeze there,
Life's silly moments laid bare.

The Serendipity of Knotted Twine

Twisted strands of fate collide,
In a tumble, we take a ride.
With each loop, a chuckle grows,
As life pulls tight, then later slows.

Unexpected knots, a playful mess,
Bring a smile, our hearts they bless.
Through tangled troubles we find cheer,
A tapestry of joy draws near.

Radiant Threads of Delight

Colors clash, a vibrant sight,
A jester's grin, so full of light.
Threads weave tales, both bright and bold,
In every stitch, a joy unrolled.

Laughter mingles with every hue,
In this fabric, old becomes new.
With every pull, a moment sings,
In the art of joy, our spirit springs.

Mirthful Patterns in the Tapestry

Patterns swirling, a comic scene,
Where colors merge, and laughter's keen.
From silly shapes, we craft our fun,
In every corner, we find the sun.

Threads of whimsy, twirls and spins,
With giggles stitched where the story begins.
A patchwork heart, so rich and bright,
Unravels joy in pure delight.

Delight in Every Loop

In a world of knots and bends,
We find joy around the trends.
Twisting tales and silly pranks,
Life's a dance; we give our thanks.

With giggles wrapped in every thread,
A tapestry where worries shred.
Come unwind, join in the cheer,
For fun resides right over here.

Each twist a tale, each turn a laugh,
We share the joy, we add the gaff.
With each new stitch, our spirits soar,
Together we craft forevermore.

Threads of Lightheartedness

In stitches bright, we weave a dream,
With playful jests, and silly themes.
Each loop a smile, each knot a play,
Brightening up a gloomy day.

With laughter spun in vibrant hues,
We share our quirks, our fun-filled views.
Tangles bring forth the best of glee,
Unraveling fun, just you and me.

Through loops and wefts, our sillies blend,
Each thread a tale that has no end.
In the fabric of joy, we find our bliss,
Embracing life with a cheerful twist.

Bursts of Joy in the Weave

A fabric rich in giggly threads,
Where whimsy dances, and laughter spreads.
Bright patterns formed by cheerful hearts,
In every weave, pure joy imparts.

With every knot, a hearty grin,
Our tangled tales begin to spin.
In bursts of joy, our craft ignites,
We paint our world with sheer delights.

Through playful loops, mishaps arise,
Turning blunders into chuckle skies.
Crafting a tapestry of pure fun,
Where every moment shines like the sun.

The Cord of Cheerfulness

A cord unspooled with laughter bright,
Entwines our days in pure delight.
Jokes and jests in every strand,
We share our joy, hand in hand.

In every twist, a silly tale,
Where happiness is sure to sail.
With fibers soft, our hearts connect,
In the warmth of smiles, we reflect.

Through fibers strong, our spirits rise,
Crafting a bond beyond the skies.
With every pull, our giggles grow,
In cheerfulness, we fully flow.

The Bright Threads of Togetherness

In the loom of our days, we weave a tale,
With colors of friendship that never grow pale.
A stitch here, a twist there, laughter takes flight,
Bright threads of connection, a joyful delight.

We gather in circles, our quirks on display,
Where giggles and winks make the mundane sway.
Each moment a patch, unique in its way,
Together we flourish, in a colorful fray.

Frayed Edges of Folly

Oh, the quirks of our actions, a comical sight,
A sock on my hand, what a silly delight!
We trip over gags, like loose threads they flee,
Frayed edges of folly, how joyful are we!

With pranks in the air, and jesters in cheer,
We dance through the mess, igniting good cheer.
In this tapestry woven, with echoes of glee,
Folly's our banner, pure jest guarantees.

The Warp and Weft of Jokes

In the warp of our stories, the punchlines take form,
Twisting and turning, like weathered old yarn.
The weft of our laughter, a fabric so bright,
With every new joke, we turn wrong into right.

We gather to share our best comedic finds,
Each rib-tickling tale, like threads intertwined.
With snorts and with giggles, we dance through the night,

A tapestry blooming in mirthful delight.

The Fabric of Joyful Mischief

In the seams of our nights, mischief takes flight,
With playful intentions, we sparkle with light.
A wink and a nudge, we unite in this scheme,
The fabric of joy, woven with laughter's dream.

From whispers of pranks to the fun that ensues,
With heartbeats alight, we embrace silly views.
Each twist in our journey, an adventure to seek,
In this vibrant tapestry, we're never quite meek.

Threads of Bubbles and Bounty

In the garden where gnomes play,
Bubbles float and drift away.
Jokes are whispered in the breeze,
Tickling leaves and swaying trees.

Merry squirrels dance on the wall,
Chasing shadows, having a ball.
Sunlight sparkles on every bloom,
Laughter echoes, dispels the gloom.

Each petal wears a cheeky grin,
As if they know where joy begins.
A giggle hides in every space,
Nature's smile, a warm embrace.

With each stitch, the day unfolds,
Funny stories in colors bold.
Crafted moments, so rich and sweet,
Life is playful, a happy treat.

Ties That Chuckle

Amidst the threads that intertwine,
Giggles burst like morning wine.
Frogs in ties and hats so bright,
Hopping forth in pure delight.

The sun winks through the curtain lace,
Inviting joy to join the chase.
With every loop and every twirl,
Life spins round, a dancing whirl.

Wooly sheep with silly hair,
Bouncing without a single care.
Their laughter bounces on the wind,
A merry tune that won't rescind.

Through every twist, a chuckle rings,
In every corner, humor sings.
Laughter binds this crafty art,
In tangled threads, we share our heart.

Giggling Along the Grain

In a forest where the sun does play,
Woodland creatures frolic all day.
Barks are grinning, trees are wide,
Nature revels, there's nothing to hide.

A rabbit wears a vest of green,
Sharing jokes that are quite obscene.
Mice on mushrooms exchange a glance,
Underneath the leaves, they prance.

Squirrels giggle from up high,
Swinging branches, reaching the sky.
Nuts drop down with a funny thud,
Creating giggles with every thud.

Sunlight dances on golden grain,
As whispers of mischief remain.
Life plays on in a silly dream,
Where joy and laughter brightly gleam.

Whimsical Weavings of the Heart

With threads of color, we spin a tale,
Of merriment that will not pale.
Every stitch tells a funny lore,
Of moments shared, who could ask for more?

Laughter wraps us in its embrace,
As playful smiles light up the space.
With every knot, a story starts,
Whimsical weavings of joyful hearts.

In the cracks of a cobbled lane,
Giggling children play in the rain.
Their laughter sparkles, fills the air,
Creating magic everywhere.

From left to right, the tapestry flows,
With silly faces that everyone knows.
A kaleidoscope of fun and cheer,
In this vibrant quilt, love draws near.

Chasing Giggles in the Weave

In threads of cheer, we dance and play,
A tapestry of jests on display.
With every twist, a chuckle's near,
We revel in joy, through laughter clear.

The looms hum softly, tales entwined,
A fabric of smiles, sweetly designed.
With playful weaves, we're lost in fun,
Chasing the giggles, we run and run.

Each knot a story, a wink, a tease,
The fibers shimmer, as laughter frees.
In every corner, jesters appear,
Crafting delight, drawing us near.

Through seams of mirth, we weave our fate,
In the quilt of joy, we celebrate.
With threads of whimsy, hearts ignite,
Chasing giggles, a pure delight.

Riddles Stitched with Sunshine

Under bright skies, we share our glee,
With riddles wrapped in warmth, we see.
Sunshine stitches in every line,
Crafting laughter, a playful design.

Each word a pattern, fun to explore,
A tapestry woven from giggles galore.
In the patchwork of thoughts, we find our way,
With riddles that dance and play all day.

Stitched with sunlight, bright as can be,
In fabric of joy, we're wild and free.
Each question sprouted, blooms in delight,
With each silly answer, the world feels right.

In threads of fun, we intertwine,
Riddles unite, hearts align.
Through playful banter, sunshine glows,
In the laughter's embrace, our happiness grows.

Laughing Through the Fiber

In a cloth of giggles, we find our place,
Every fiber holds a smiling face.
Through delicate strands, laughter flows,
In the fabric of fun, anything goes.

With each silly twist, a new tale is spun,
Laughter echoing like rays of the sun.
In the weave of our hearts, jokes take flight,
Conversations that shimmer, spark, and excite.

Crafting connections in playful ways,
Through knots of humor, we brighten our days.
With laughter as needle, and joy as the thread,
Sewing memories cherished, never misread.

Every stitch a smile, every seam a next,
In the fabric of life, we find what's perplexed.
Weaving together, laughter entwined,
Through fibers of joy, our hearts aligned.

The Joyful Entanglement

In the web of mischief, we find delight,
Threads of laughter, dancing in light.
With knots of confusion, but laughter that springs,
In joyful entanglement, joy always clings.

Each twist brings a giggle, a funny surprise,
A tapestry woven with bright, happy eyes.
In the chaos of thread, we find our groove,
As laughter and fun together, we move.

Embracing the tangle, we leap with glee,
Through moments of whimsy, wild and free.
In the weaving of joy, let's dive deep,
With threads of laughter, our hearts we keep.

Entangled we are, in love and in cheer,
Every stitch a memory, precious and dear.
Through the fabric of life, in giggles we dwell,
In the joyful entanglement, all is well.

Tapestry of Tickles

In a garden of giggles, blooms surprise,
Threads of joy dance, beneath the skies.
Whimsical patterns, zigzag and twirl,
Every corner winks, with a playful swirl.

Laughter spills over, like champagne's cheer,
Silly shadows prance, drawing us near.
Each stitch a story, spun with delight,
Weaving together our hearts so light.

Beneath a sky painted with humor's hue,
Kites of jest soar, on the breezy blue.
The sunshine chuckles, tickling the air,
In this patchwork haven, worries lay bare.

With every reminder, laughter's embrace,
The joy in the weave, we cannot replace.
A tapestry rich, where silliness blends,
In this merry fabric, the fun never ends.

The Weave of Whimsy

A jester's delight spins round and round,
Patterns of mischief in joy we have found.
With every twist, the fibers unite,
Creating a canvas, oh what a sight!

Threads that shimmer with giggles and glee,
Swaying like dancers, oh come join me!
Tangles of laughter, all tied in a knot,
In this eccentric loom, we've crafted a lot.

Each fiber whispers a tale of surprise,
Dreams intertwined beneath twinkling skies.
We pull on the strands, laughter ignites,
Beneath the fabric, the spirit alights.

Here in this maze woven thick with delight,
Whimsical echoes put hearts in flight.
A delightful creation, both funny and fine,
In this playful weave, we joyfully dine.

Melodies of Mirth in Every Stitch

In every seam, a chuckle resides,
Each note of joy in the fabric abides.
A melody woven, a playful refrain,
Lifting our spirits, like sunshine after rain.

With needles of humor, we dance and we play,
Crafting our tales in a light-hearted way.
Every thread sings a tune so sweet,
In this joyous crafting, our hearts skip a beat.

The rhythm of laughter, a playful song,
In the tapestry's weave, we all belong.
Swirls of delight in each little seam,
A quilt stitched tight, like a whimsical dream.

With every twist and a jolly twirl,
Life's little joys, like a bright whirling pearl.
In the fabric of merriment, we find our bliss,
Each stitch a promise, of joy and of kiss.

Grins Within the Gossamer

A whisper of laughter drifts in the air,
Gossamer threads in a dance without care.
Tangled in smiles, the fabric reveals,
Jests that awaken, and charm that appeals.

In a web of delight, where echoes play,
Silly faces bloom, brightening the day.
The glow of joy wraps around every heart,
In this intricacy, we each play a part.

Laughter like rain on a sun-kissed morn,
Glistens like dew on the grass freshly shorn.
Each moment we share, a sparkle, a gift,
In this delicate weave, our spirits uplift.

With every heartbeat, a chuckle takes flight,
Tales intertwined, a magical sight.
In the world we create with gossamer grace,
Smiles blossom freely, finding their place.

Harmony in the Handcrafted

In a world of threads so fine,
Jokes dance like stars that shine.
Stitches whisper secrets low,
Crafted tales that surely flow.

Each knot a laugh, each twist a grin,
Patterns weave where fun begins.
Colors clash, a jolly spree,
Handcrafted joys, wild and free.

A patch of clumsy, a seam so bright,
Laughter blooms, a pure delight.
From needle's tip, a giggle sings,
Crafts conceal the joy it brings.

So gather round this merry quilt,
With every square, let worries wilt.
In handmade joys, new bonds are found,
With harmony, we're tightly bound.

Humor Woven with Care

Threads of laughter in our hands,
Crafting joy in merry bands.
Bobbins filled with stories sweet,
Woven tales beneath our feet.

Needles dance and fingers fly,
Tickling dreams as moments sigh.
Fabric folds, a giggle's tune,
Stitched up bright as afternoon.

Each turn reveals a playful spark,
In shadows hid, we leave our mark.
Laughter spun, for all to wear,
Humor tangled, light as air.

So come and join this vibrant weave,
In every stitch, there's joy to achieve.
With every cut, with every seam,
Life's a patchwork, fun's the dream.

Playful Patterns in the Fabric

Bright designs across the cloth,
Tickled shades, they spark our growth.
Wobbly lines, a crooked laugh,
Patchwork smiles in every half.

Dancing colors spin and sway,
Creating giggles in the fray.
Threaded tales of cheer unfold,
In playful patterns, memories hold.

Silly prints and winking seams,
We stitch together joyful dreams.
Fraying edges, yet we cheer,
Lifted spirits gathering near.

So embrace the quirks, let's entwine,
In fabric fun, our hearts align.
With each new piece, our laughter grows,
In vibrant threads, our story flows.

Worries Untangled with a Smile

Knot the fears, we've found the thread,
In fabric fun, our hearts are fed.
Tangled thoughts unravel slow,
With every laugh, we start to glow.

Crafting comforts, light and free,
Laughter's balm, a sweet decree.
In quirky seams and patterned cheer,
Worries fade when friends are near.

Embroidered dreams will take their place,
With every twist, joy finds its pace.
Bright patterns help us ease the grind,
In playful stitches, peace we find.

So gather round, weave tales of cheer,
Each story shared, we hold so dear.
With smiles stitched in every seam,
Let's quilt our worries, live the dream.

Patterns of Play in the Fabric

In threads of joy, we spin and twine,
With nimble fingers, we cross the line.
Each stitch a giggle, each seam a grin,
A tapestry blooms where fun begins.

With colors bright, our laughter tracks,
A patchwork party, no room for hacks.
Every loop and knot, a story unfurls,
In this woven world, delight whirls.

We frolic between the warp and weft,
Crafting gags, oh what a deft!
The fabric hums with sweet delight,
As playful spirits take their flight.

So join the dance, pull patterns anew,
In this clever craft, there's much to view.
From silliness sewn, joy does erupt,
In the fabric of fun, we are all construct.

Chronicles of Chortles

Gather round the tales we weave,
Of foolish fables, who'd believe?
With every snicker, a page is turned,
In the chronicles, light hearts are earned.

Adventures unfold in snappy prose,
Where slip-ups sprout like dandelion grows.
Each hiccup and blunder, a gem to find,
In our joyful saga, we're intertwined.

The humor blooms in space between,
Where smiles dance, absurdity seen.
A quirky plot, rich and bold,
Beneath the laughter, stories unfold.

So turn the leaf, let the chuckles spark,
In the light of joy, we leave our mark.
With every giggle, memories form,
In this book of merriment, hearts stay warm.

Weaving Smiles into Memories

With every thread, a smile is sewn,
A tapestry grand, of laughter grown.
Stitches of joy, across the span,
Each twirl and twist, the fun began.

Moments captured in fiber's embrace,
Funny incidents put in their place.
In the fabric of life, mischief breathes,
Sailing on sails of whimsical wreathed.

So lift your spirits, let humor glide,
In every woven tale, we take pride.
We knit convivial times, never to fray,
Smiles woven firmly, come what may.

With a needle of humor and thread of cheer,
We craft a legacy that draws us near.
Memories blooming, a garden we maintain,
In the quilt of our lives, laughter's the gain.

The Embroidery of Ecstasy

In subtle stitches, joy is outlined,
Whimsical patterns that bind and unwind.
Beneath each loop, giggles nestle tight,
In this splendid craft, everything feels right.

Embroidery dances, bright and bold,
Mixing emotions, stories told.
Each knot a chuckle, each thread a grin,
In this vibrant art, happiness spins.

Crafted with care, in colors so bright,
We gather our woes, crafting delight.
From tales of folly to joyous recalls,
In this masterwork, every spirit enthralls.

So hold your needles, let laughter flow,
In our merry dance, together we grow.
The fabric of life, stitched with glee,
In the embroidery of ecstasy, we're free.

Colors of Chuckles in the Weave

In the tapestry of giggles, bright,
The threads of whimsy twist in light.
Every stitch a smile, every knot a grin,
A patchwork of joy where laughs begin.

Crazy patterns, swirling round,
A dance of jest where fun is found.
Colors burst, a vivid spree,
Where every hue holds mystery.

Jesters prance in every thread,
Whispering secrets, joy widespread.
In the fabric, all fears untie,
With every chuckle, spirits fly.

So let the quilt of mirth unfold,
In every corner, laughter bold.
Wrap yourself in this delight,
Where joy is woven, day and night.

Bonds of Humor in the Fabrication

In the seams of smiles, we gather close,
Threads of friendship, where laughter flows.
With every tickle, bonds entwine,
Crafting joy, a design divine.

Quirky patchwork, stitched with care,
In this creation, secrets we share.
Every tear a tale, every fray a jest,
In the fabric of humor, we're truly blessed.

Witty knots hold tight the fun,
In this canvas, our hearts are one.
The weaver's hands dance with delight,
Crafting chuckles from day to night.

Come join the thread that never snaps,
In our fabric, let's share the laughs.
With every stitch, our spirits soar,
Creating memories, forevermore.

Swaying in a Symphony of Glee

In the rhythm of giggles, we sway,
Notes of laughter fill the day.
With every chuckle, melodies rise,
Harmonies twinkle in brightened eyes.

The canvas of joy, brushed with fun,
Strumming heartstrings, one by one.
Each verse sings in playful cheer,
Creating echoes we hold dear.

Dancing shadows, playfully tease,
In this symphony, we do as we please.
With every chuckle, a softer tune,
Harmony whispers beneath the moon.

So come and join this merry throng,
In the music of laughter, we belong.
As the joy flows deep in our stride,
Let the symphony be our guide.

Fractals of Joy in the Mesh

In the web of smiles, we find our way,
Fractals of joy brighten the gray.
Every corner holds a playful cheer,
In this mesh, laughter draws near.

Patterns twist in fanciful flight,
Echoing chuckles, pure delight.
Each loop and weave, a playful sign,
Where the divine meets the silly line.

Woven deeply, our spirits blend,
In this tapestry, the giggles never end.
Every fiber a burst of bliss,
Moments like these, we do not miss.

So let the mesh stretch wide and free,
In the fractals, find your glee.
As we dive into the playful throng,
Spinning tales where we all belong.

Playful Yarns of Yesterday

In twilight's glow, we'd weave our tales,
With giggles trapped like tiny gales.
A kite that flew, an ice cream spill,
Each moment crafted with joyful thrill.

Our games were wild, our feet were bare,
We danced like leaves in the summer air.
Each secret shared behind the trees,
Brought laughter floating on the breeze.

From silly pranks to whispered dreams,
We stitched our bond with silly schemes.
With every giggle, we felt so free,
In playful yarns, just you and me.

Now memories shimmer like a prize,
Reflecting joy in our near-sighted eyes.
Though time may stretch and years may fade,
The laughter remains, forever displayed.

Mirthful Fabrics of Friendship

A tapestry spun of whispers and cheer,
Where every thread draws friends near.
With fondness bright, in colors bold,
We share our lives, our tales retold.

With puns and jests, our hearts we warm,
In the twist and turn, we find our charm.
A patchwork quilt of silly schemes,
We stitch together our wildest dreams.

Through snickers light and playful fights,
We find our spark in simple nights.
In mirthful bonds, we surely thrive,
For laughter's echoes help us survive.

So here's to us, a jolly crew,
With smiles that twinkle like morning dew.
In friendship's fabric, we've found our place,
In swirling joy, we gently embrace.

The Understanding Weave of Smiles

A thread of joy in daily grind,
Where smiles emerge, our hearts aligned.
With knowing glances, we share the fun,
A weave of laughter, second to none.

We paint the days with silly talk,
As shadows dance on our evening walk.
The jokes unfold in perfect time,
In bonding moments, pure and prime.

Through ups and downs, we've spun this thread,
In every giggle, new joys are bred.
A fabric rich with warmth and care,
The understanding weave is always there.

So let us cherish this playful knot,
In life's grand quilt, we've crafted a lot.
For smiles are treasures that never fade,
In the tapestry of moments we've made.

Threads of Happiness Tightly Wound

In a circle of friends, the laughter grows,
Like tiny rivers where joy freely flows.
A fabric made of running gags,
Stitc hed tightly with fun-filled brags.

With jests as light as a feather's touch,
We weave our stories, and oh, how much!
With every stitch, there's magic spun,
In threads of happiness, our hearts are one.

In silly dances and whispered news,
We share our secrets, we share our blues.
Around the loom, we spin and twirl,
Crafting happiness in a bright, warm whirl.

The threads may fray, but never tear,
For in each knot, there's love to spare.
So let us weave till day is done,
In a tapestry where we all have fun.

Joyful Constellations in the Loom

A stitch here, a knot there, laughter flies,
Twirling threads that dance and rise.
Patterns bright like stars at night,
They shimmer with pure delight.

The needle's wink, a playful tease,
Woven tales that aim to please.
Giggles caught in every seam,
Creating our wildest dream.

With colors bold, we spin and sway,
In the loom, we find our play.
Tangled joy in every hue,
A canvas of the funny, too.

So let us weave our tales so grand,
With each loop, a gentle hand.
In this fabric, laughter thrives,
A tapestry of joyful lives.

Tapestries of Tickle and Triumph

In every thread, a joke is sown,
A tickle here, a triumph grown.
With each pull and twist of yarn,
We craft a world, both bright and warm.

Patterns dance like springtime's breeze,
Joyful whispers among the leaves.
Each knot a giggle, every weave,
Unraveling shapes that we believe.

A tapestry of heart and cheer,
Where every stitch is full of beer!
For every loop, a tale unfolds,
In colors bold, our laughter holds.

So grab your thread, join in the fun,
With laughter's glow, the work begun.
In this tapestry, we shall find,
The spirits lifted, hearts entwined.

Whispers of Joy Between the Threads

Beneath the strands, where shadows play,
Whispers of joy guide the way.
The loom hums a cheerful tune,
As laughter twirls, a carefree balloon.

Dancing fibers, brightly spun,
With every jest, we come undone.
Threads intertwined, a riot of cheer,
Gleaning giggles that draw us near.

With needles clicking, fun ignites,
In this weave, pure delight excites.
Giggles echo, fill the air,
A celebration beyond compare.

Among the threads, we find our peace,
In every stitch, a moment's ease.
Together we craft our joyful art,
A patchwork quilt of every heart.

Giggles in the Garden of Connections

In a garden where laughter grows,
Each flower blooms with silly shows.
Petals tickle with every breeze,
Creating smiles, if you please.

Twisting vines like playful frowns,
We share our joy; it knows no bounds.
With every bloom, a laugh takes flight,
Transforming day into pure delight.

The sun shines bright on merry sights,
As we stitch dreams with all our might.
Caterpillars giggle, butterflies sing,
In our garden, joy is a spring.

So wander through these fields of cheer,
With every step, let warmth draw near.
In this patch of laughter and light,
Connections thrive; it feels so right.

Smiles Knotted into Nature

In the garden, giggles bloom,
Petals painted with joy's perfume.
Bumblebees buzz, dance in delight,
As butterflies flutter, a colorful sight.

A squirrel steals acorns, plays hide and seek,
Tickling the branches, laughter unique.
Leaves rustle softly, whispers of fun,
Nature's own jest, under the sun.

Raindrops tap on the window's frame,
Each plink a joke, part of the game.
The sun peeks out, wearing a grin,
Chasing away clouds, inviting kin.

With every breeze, the trees sway and sway,
Telling tall tales in a playful way.
Nature's own giggle, a symphony bright,
Creating chuckles from morning to night.

Riddles Among the Ribbing

A worm winks from the rich, soft ground,
With riddles of laughter, all around.
The sun says, 'Why is a crow black?'
'Because it's the best at hiding its snack!'

In bushes, a rabbit rolls in the grass,
Wearing a hat made of leaves—what a class!
He nibbles on carrots with such great flair,
While toads croak jokes that float in the air.

Each stone has a story, each crack a pun,
Whispers of humor in shadows they spun.
The brook sings a ballad, water's sweet tease,
As frogs leap to dance in a splashy breeze.

Beneath the tall trees, giggles entwine,
The bark sticks a tongue out, just to define.
With every creak, and every small bump,
The forest is filled with a whimsical thump.

The Stitches of Sweetness

In a quilt of delight, stories are sewn,
Each patch a giggle, never alone.
A cat naps in threads, soft and sweet,
Dreaming of fish that dance on their feet.

Buttons of laughter, they bounce and play,
Stitching together the clouds of the day.
The sun beams in, casting warmth all around,
As giggles and glee in each corner are found.

A patchwork of whispers, secrets that glow,
Woven with joy, oh what a show!
With every stitch, used yarn turns bright,
Creating a tapestry of pure delight.

With needles that leap like frogs in a race,
Every little loop holds a smile on its face.
Threads tangled in fun, a marvelous sight,
Knots of sweet chuckles, a fabric of light.

Fun in the Fray

Amidst the hustle, bustling in play,
Chaos is charming, come what may.
A jester crow flits with a wink,
As the world spins round, don't you think?

In the midst of the fray, there's joy to be found,
Socks that don't match dance on the ground.
A picnic of giggles, each crumb a cheer,
Spilled lemonade, laughter so near.

Sidewalks are rivers where puddles bloom,
Splashing through joy, dispelling all gloom.
The wind tells secrets to daisies and bees,
While children all topple like leaves in the breeze.

With wobbly bikes and squeaky shoes,
Every silly stumble gives laughter its dues.
In the heart of the fray, where mishaps reside,
We find our delight, in the joyous ride.

Sunshine Stitched into the Weave

In the fabric of the day, they play,
Threads of giggles twirl and sway.
Colors burst, a canvas bright,
Smiles break forth in pure delight.

Tangles form in silly knots,
Our laughter dances, connects the dots.
Tickles weave through every seam,
Awakening joy, a sunny dream.

Each stitch a tale of playful cheer,
Woven memories, oh-so-dear.
Patterns formed by happy hands,
Creating magic in the strands.

So when the day gets rather bland,
Reach for humor, take a stand.
In this tapestry we find our bliss,
A world spun with a giggly twist.

Fables of Fun Interlaced

In the storybook of vibrant threads,
Witty whispers fill our heads.
Each tale a wink, a playful tease,
Crafting smiles with effortless ease.

Characters dance in quirky style,
With every twist, they make us smile.
A zany crew, forever bold,
Their laughter's worth its weight in gold.

From mischievous gnomes to silly elves,
They teach us joy is found in selves.
Each plot unfolds in giggly ways,
Turning mundane to bright sunrays.

So gather 'round, let's share a jest,
In these fables, we're truly blessed.
For humor's threads bind us tight,
Turning days into pure delight.

Joyful Threads Amongst the Tangled

Amidst the chaos of life's weave,
Joyful threads begin to cleave.
Snags and twists might cause a fuss,
But laughter shines, it's quite a plus.

With playful pokes and teasing jabs,
We turn our woes to silly blabs.
In every tangle, a twist awaits,
A chance to giggle, oh how great!

Our yarns may knot, our fibers bend,
Yet through the mess, our spirits mend.
Together we weave with hearts so light,
Transforming blunders to pure delight.

So when the threads seem worn and fray,
Let laughter guide the way we play.
For tangled joy is what we seek,
In every chuckle, we find our peak.

The Cheery Net of Connection

A net of joy, spun with delight,
Catching moments, oh so bright.
Each mesh a smile, each knot a cheer,
Bringing together those who are dear.

In this web where laughter brews,
Silly stories come alive in hues.
Friends entwined, a merry crowd,
Their giggles rise, joyful and loud.

The strands that bond us twist and twine,
Creating memories, sweet as wine.
In every corner, warmth unfolds,
Through shared chuckles, our tale is told.

So grasp the net, don't let it slip,
On this frolicsome friendship trip.
In laughter's grip, we thrive and grow,
In this cheery web, joy's seeds we sow.

Peals of Laughter in the Weave

In the fabric of the day, there's a twist,
Where giggles mingle, cannot be missed.
Threads of humor dance in the sun,
Each stitch a secret, each knot a pun.

As shadows play tricks, the moments unfold,
With stories retold, both funny and bold.
Patchwork of joy wraps the world so bright,
In every corner, there's a burst of light.

With a wink from the weaver, a chuckle is spun,
Each fiber a tale; oh, isn't it fun?
Tapestries twist, giving laughter a home,
In the boundless vast, where giggles roam.

Frolicsome threads in the loom that we weave,
In every misstep, there's a reason to believe.
Life's quilt is crafted with whimsy, my friend,
Hold on tight to the laughter; it never will end.

Whimsy Between Woven Lines

A jester's cap hangs on a clever thread,
Tickles and giggles in each word said.
Woven in whispers, the fabric sways,
Curly jokes flutter in comical ways.

In the seams of the day, surprises appear,
Puns and jests fill the atmosphere.
From knots of mirth, we untie the fun,
As life's little puzzles invite everyone.

Needles of laughter stitch moments anew,
A tapestry bright with a vibrant hue.
Waves of delight brush the fabric so grand,
In the playful art of a master hand.

So gather round, let the stories unite,
In the patchwork of joy, everything's right.
In the dance of the threads, we find our way,
With merriment woven in a brilliant array.

The Framework of Folly

In corners of chaos, where laughter does grow,
A framework of folly begins to show.
With every mistake, we dance and we cheer,
For humor and kindness make everything clear.

Posts of odd stories stand tall and proud,
Echoes of laughter can gather a crowd.
With beams of delight, we shape our own fate,
Where whimsy and giggles refuse to be late.

All the blunders become badges we wear,
In the great scheme of life, we learn to share.
The architecture of chuckles frames our delight,
In this world of wonder, we soar to new height.

As moments unfold in this playful embrace,
Each line we create holds a smile on its face.
So gather together, let's build and explore,
In the framework of folly, there's always much more.

Tied Together by Joy

With ribbons of laughter, we weave our dreams,
In a tapestry bright, bursting at the seams.
Every twist and turn adds to the fun,
Binding our hearts 'til the day is done.

In a world of zany, we jump and we spin,
Finding delight in the silly within.
The threads of our friendship are woven so tight,
In every shared giggle, we shine oh so bright.

Tangles may come, but we laugh through the fray,
In the dance of the stitches, we learn how to play.
With every mishap, a new tale is spun,
Together we sparkle, oh yes, we are one.

So let's hoot and holler, embrace every part,
For joy is the thread that connects every heart.
In this grand little quilt, may our laughter resound,
Tied together by joy, in happiness found.

The Fabric of Merriment

Threads of joy in every seam,
Stitching up a playful dream.
With every knot, a giggle shared,
Laughter floats on breezes aired.

Patterns dance with cheerful glee,
Woven tales for you and me.
Colors burst in vibrant cheer,
Tickling hearts when friends are near.

Fabrics shimmer with silly sights,
Draped in warmth of playful nights.
Every fiber tells a joke,
In this quilt where whimsy pokes.

So come and wrap in threads of fun,
Together, we can laugh as one.
In every stitch, a smile's spun,
A tapestry where joy's begun.

Gleeful Weavings Beneath the Surface

Underneath each cheerful stitch,
Winks of laughter, oh so rich.
Patterns gleam with secrets planned,
Ticklish whispers in the hand.

Nestled close, the colors play,
Mixing bright with shades of gray.
Knots of joy, undone at times,
Twisted yarns tell silly rhymes.

In the weave, a crowing jest,
Beneath the layers, laughter rests.
Silly moments, stitched so tight,
Bubbling up with pure delight.

Come explore this quilted spree,
Where every twist is jubilee.
With threads of warmth, our hearts align,
In this fabric, joy will shine.

Smiles Interlaced with Dreams

In the threads where giggles hide,
Dreams are woven, side by side.
Every tale a tapestry,
Wit and whimsy wild and free.

Smiles cascade like streams of gold,
In every fold, a story told.
Knitted jokes and playful gleams,
Stitched together, oh how it beams!

From the fabric, chuckles rise,
Winding through like butterflies.
In this cloth, the humor's bright,
Turning gloom to sheer delight.

So join the dance of winks and grins,
In woven realms, the fun begins.
With every loop, a chance to play,
Keep the dreariness at bay.

Jests Among the Woven Branches

Among the threads, a jester waits,
Sipping tea from laughing plates.
With every twist, a quip released,
Crafting chuckles, joy increased.

Branches stretch with whimsy's might,
Dancing gently in the light.
Leaves of green with giggles spun,
Playful whispers, oh what fun!

Beneath the bark, a secret joke,
Wrapped in warmth, it can provoke.
Every fiber a punchline bold,
Woven tales of mirth unfold.

So gather round this lively tree,
Let's share the smiles, you and me.
In woven shades of joy we'll bask,
Jests entwined, no need to ask.

Patterns of Positivity

In the garden of giggles, where smiles bloom bright,
Jokes tumble like leaves, what a comical sight.
Each thread spun with joy, in a tapestry grand,
Friendship's warm colors, together we stand.

Wit dances like fireflies, twinkling with glee,
Tickles and chuckles, as light as can be.
The patterns we weave, in threads of delight,
Create joyful moments that sparkle at night.

Life's clown with a wink, jests on the way,
Unraveling worries, come what may.
In this fabric of fun, we find our release,
A patchwork of laughter, a moment's peace.

So gather your friends, let the silliness flow,
With giggles and grins, let your true colors show.
In this bright quilt of joy, we endlessly spin,
Each stitch filled with humor; let the fun begin.

Lively Weavings of Laughter

On a shuttle of jokes, we sail through the day,
Winding through stories, where grins come out to play.
Each twist is a chuckle, each turn a delight,
As we stitch up our tales, shining ever so bright.

Banters like ribbons, stream through the air,
Colors of humor are wondrously rare.
We craft a mosaic of silliness bold,
Spun tales that shimmer, in warm hues of gold.

In corners of cheer, the merry threads twine,
Creating a canvas where funny is fine.
The best jokes are woven, in moments we share,
Sprinkling joy's essence, dissolving all care.

So snuggle up close, with laughter we bind,
In this lively creation, good vibes you'll find.
With every soft stitch, our spirits take flight,
In weavings of joy, we shine through the night.

The Loom of Lighthearted Tales

In a world woven tight with whimsical yarns,
Tales twist and turn with their playful charms.
The loom spins its magic, with each hearty laugh,
Creating a fabric that brings joy by the half.

A jester's bright giggle, a wink and a nod,
In patterns of mischief, we're all a bit flawed.
With every light step, and a wink in the eye,
Our stories take flight like birds in the sky.

The colors of mirth dance in playful embrace,
Jumbles of joy found in every space.
So gather your dreams, and weave them with care,
In this lovely tapestry, let's all take our share.

So hand-in-hand let's tread, with laughter our guide,
In this loom of delight, let's joyously ride.
Each thread holds a moment, each weave tells a tale,
In the fabric of fun, we'll always prevail.

A Stitch in Time Holds Laughter

A needle of fun stitches bright in the day,
Crafting little quirks in a clever ballet.
With threads spun from smiles and moments abloom,
We patch up the grayness and brighten the room.

We twine together quirks that keep us alive,
In vibrant connections, our spirits will thrive.
Each knot a new memory, each loop a delight,
In the heart of our fabric, we twinkle so bright.

With each playful jab, we unearth hidden cheer,
Embracing the giggles that everyone hears.
A bouquet of laughter that keeps growing strong,
In the quilt of our journeys, all where we belong.

So let's thread our adventures, with joy intertwined,
In this vivid creation, happiness aligned.
With warm stitches of friendship, we'll never unwind,
In this lovely design, true joy we will find.

The Interlace of Delight

Amid the threads of merry spree,
We twist and turn, so wild and free.
With every knot, a chuckle grows,
In this fine web, silliness flows.

A jester's cap upon my head,
Dancing joyfully where I tread.
With every twirl and playful glance,
We stumble on in a silly dance.

Giggling gusts blow through our minds,
Unraveling thoughts that laughter finds.
In woven strands of gleeful cheer,
The lightness lifts us—far and near.

Together woven, side by side,
In this bright fabric, we'll abide.
For in the mesh where joy is found,
Our hearts and laughter spin around.

Silliness in the Silk

In shadows where the gleeful spin,
Soft silk reminds of the grins within.
Tangles, twists, a light refrain,
Each fiber hums a merry gain.

A playful prance, a sudden trip,
We craft our joy, with winks and quips.
Threads of humor stretch so wide,
We sew our giggles side by side.

With every fiber pulled tight,
We weave a dream of pure delight.
In every slip, a joyful cheer,
Our hearts in unison, ever near.

The warmth of laughter, soft and bright,
In this silk cocoon, we take flight.
For joy entwined is what we seek,
In the silliness, we find our peak.

A Tangle of Elation

In knots we're bound, yet oh so free,
A tangle of joy, just you and me.
With every loop, a chuckle shared,
In the mess of life, we're unprepared.

What if the world's a playful jest?
In each mishap, we find the best.
The more we trip, the more we grin,
In this wild maze, we both win.

A hint of chaos, a splash of cheer,
Our laughter rings, it's music dear.
In every twist, a story told,
With silliness, our hearts behold.

As we embrace each frolicsome fight,
Our tangled paths feel ever right.
In this jumbled thread, we relate,
With joyful spirits that never abate.

The Texture of Happiness

A threadbare smile, a soft embrace,
In this warm weave, we find our place.
Each fiber whispers sweet, sweet bliss,
In the fine fabric of each laugh and kiss.

Patterns of joy in every seam,
A patch of giggles, a playful dream.
Frolic some more, let worries fade,
In this quilt of laughter, we wade.

With every stitch, we chase the gloom,
Reviving spirits in the room.
Each playful flick of fabric bright,
Crafting delight, our hearts take flight.

So weave your laughter, let it fly,
In the texture of happiness, hello high!
With our hearts strung tight in harmony,
We find the joy in absurdity.

Playful Stitches of Life

In a world where threads entwine,
We dance and fumble, oh so fine.
Each twist and turn brings giggles forth,
Creating joy and endless mirth.

A sprinkle here, a stitch that's bold,
Unraveled tales of laughter told.
With every pull, we find the cheer,
In every seam, a chuckle near.

In pockets deep, surprises hide,
A silly grin we cannot bide.
With laughter rippling through each line,
The fabric of our lives, divine.

So gather 'round this quilt so bright,
Where playful threads dance in the light.
With mischief sewn into each fold,
We share a warmth, a joy untold.

Yarns of Whimsy and Wonder

In baskets full of colors rare,
Each strand a story, light as air.
We weave our dreams with thread so fine,
Creating worlds where chuckles shine.

A playful knot, a twist so sly,
To catch a giggle passing by.
With every pull, a tale takes flight,
In vibrant hues, our hearts unite.

So spin the wheel of joy and play,
Where whimsy weaves the mundane away.
Each loop and turn, a reason to cheer,
In every fiber, warmth draws near.

The laughter echoes in the room,
As colors dance and flowers bloom.
In joyous knots, our hearts do find,
The magic threads that tie mankind.

Embracing the Unraveled

When life unravels, we just grin,
For mischief lies where threads begin.
With every tangle, joy finds a way,
To stitch together bits of play.

A twist, a turn, a snappy jest,
In chaos found, we laugh the best.
Through frayed edges, we'll embrace,
The silliness of every case.

In tangled yarn, a treasure hides,
The quirky ways our humor rides.
As colors clash, we come alive,
In funky threads, our spirits thrive.

So here's to knots that bind us tight,
With laughter echoing through the night.
In every loop, we celebrate,
The joyful dance we conjure, mate.

Laughter Nested in the Corners

In corners deep, where shadows play,
Laughter hides, come out to stay.
We seek the joy in every seam,
In soft-spun threads, we find our dream.

A patch of whimsy waits to cheer,
With giggles lurking, drawing near.
Each quirk and quibble, wrapped in thread,
Turns ordinary to joy instead.

With playful winks and jests that shine,
In cozy nooks, where hearts entwine.
The world awash in hues so bright,
In every stitch, we weave delight.

So gather 'round, let laughter swell,
In hidden corners, tales do dwell.
With every yarn, our spirits soar,
Creating bonds forevermore.

Chuckles Amidst the Intertwine

In the garden where shadows play,
Silly stories dance and sway.
Giggling leaves in a gentle breeze,
Whispers of joy from the buzzing bees.

Twists and turns of woven cheer,
Even the crows join in the sphere.
With each knot, a new tale spins,
In laughter's grasp, our joy begins.

Wiry moments, bright and spry,
Flipping hats that flutter by.
Tickled petals in merry delight,
Gurgling giggles take to flight.

When the sun dips low in the west,
Nature's jesters bring out their best.
In tangled roots, the chuckles rise,
A tapestry of fun 'neath the skies.

Jests in the Twisted Fibers

Woven threads in a merry dance,
Each fiber spinning a silly chance.
Tangled patterns, oh what a sight,
Whimsical whispers bloom with delight.

The fabric hums a playful tune,
Chasing shadows beneath the moon.
Quirky stitches in a line so bright,
Jokes abound in the soft twilight.

Snapping twine with a wink and grin,
Each fray a place where fun begins.
Fringes laughing in a silly show,
Wobbly yarns all set to go.

In the seams where the laughs entwine,
Every bend brings a quirky sign.
Gags and giggles in the textured weave,
Stories that sparkle and never leave.

Threads of Amusement

Tangled up in a world of jest,
Each little fiber feels so blessed.
Knots that giggle, colors that gleam,
Weaving wonders into a dream.

Sewn together with smiles and care,
Patchwork moments float in the air.
Jumpsuits of humor hang on the line,
Every stitch pops with a punchline.

The playful threads twist and shout,
Bouncing around without a doubt.
Loop-de-loops in a merry spin,
Life's little fables shine from within.

Fabrics of joy wrapped ever tight,
Shimmering bright in the fading light.
With cheerful patterns, we start anew,
Threads of laughter to guide us through.

Joyful Jumbles in the Fabric of Life

In the quilt where giggles are sewn,
Every patch tells a tale of our own.
Bright colors clash, a riotous flair,
Life's a circus, a joyful affair.

Stitch by stitch, we weave and twist,
Turning the mundane into bliss.
Giggles hide in the tiniest seam,
A carnival inside every dream.

Yarns entangle, mischief abounds,
As the merry laughter circling sounds.
Every quirk in the weave of fate,
Brings a smile, it's never too late.

Though the threads may fray and fade,
The joy in our hearts will never trade.
In this fabric, forever we thrive,
Jumbled happiness keeps us alive.

www.ingramcontent.com/pod-product-compliance
Lightning Source LLC
Chambersburg PA
CBHW051637160426
43209CB00004B/683